A LOOK AT WEATHER

THUNDER AND LIGHTNING

BY KATE MIKOLEY

Gareth Stevens PUBLISHING

CRASHCOURSE

Please visit our website, www.garethstevens.com. For a free color catalog of all our high-quality books, call toll free 1-800-542-2595 or fax 1-877-542-2596.

Cataloging-in-Publication Data

Names: Mikoley, Kate.
Title: Thunder and lightning / Kate Mikoley.
Description: New York : Gareth Stevens Publishing, 2024. | Series: A look at weather| Includes glossary, index, and bibliographic information
Identifiers: ISBN 9781538287378 (pbk) | ISBN 9781538287385 (library bound) | ISBN 9781538287392 (ebook)
Subjects: LCSH: Lightning-- Juvenile literature | Thunder--Juvenile literature | Storms--Juvenile literatrue
Classification: LCC QC966.5 M55 2024 | DDC 551. 56--dc24

First Edition

Published in 2024 by
Gareth Stevens Publishing
2544 Clinton Street
Buffalo, NY 14224

Designer: Karen Quigley
Editor: Kate Mikoley

Photo credits: Cover, p. 1 Den Rozhnovsky/Shutterstock.com; cloud background pp. 2-3, 32-33 kzww/Shutterstock.com; lightning background series art (lightning background) IgorZh/Shutterstock.com; series art (warm/cold front symbols) NickJulia/Shutterstock.com; series art (cloud background) ekapol sirachainan/Shutterstock.com; series art (cloud cartoon) MimaCZ/Shutterstock.com; p. 5 nexus 7/Shutterstock.com; p. 7 Suzanne Tucker/Shutterstock.com; pp. 9, 23 NOAA Weather in Focus Photo Contest 2015/photolib.noaa.gov/; p. 11 Krister462 - Fear (by-sa)/commons.wikimedia.org; p. 13 LightningBranches/commons.wikimedia.org; p. 15 Lightning over Padre Island/commons.wikimedia.org; p. 17 peterschreiber.media/Shutterstock.com; p. 19 Artemis I Prelaunch (NHQ202208270010)/commons.wikimedia.org; p. 21 Lightning striking near bridge/photolib.noaa.gov; p. 25 2021_08_10_LMA-7474/www.flickr.com/photos/noaanssl; p. 27 Tomás Guardia Bencomo/istockphoto.com; p. 29 Lauriane_Galtier_Sioux_Falls_Iowa_USA/commons.wikimedia.org; p. 30 (lightning bolts) FARBAI/Shutterstock.com.

Printed in the United States of America

Some of the images in this book illustrate individuals who are models. The depictions do not imply actual situations or events.

CPSIA compliance information: Batch #CS24GS: For further information contact Gareth Stevens at 1-800-542-2595.

CONTENTS

Words in the glossary appear in **bold** type the first time they are used in the text.

THE START OF A STORM

The rain is tapping on the ground. It's the middle of the day, but it's dark outside. Suddenly there is a big flash of light followed by a low **rumbling** sound. Here comes a thunderstorm!

Make the Grade

A thunderstorm is a storm with thunder and lightning. Whether you see it or not, all thunderstorms have lightning.

The air and gases around Earth make up something called the atmosphere. When hot, wet air quickly moves up to cooler parts of the atmosphere, thunderstorms can happen. As the hot air cools, clouds form. Rain starts to happen too.

Make the Grade

Pieces of ice called hail sometimes fall from the clouds during thunderstorms.

LEARN ABOUT LIGHTNING

Lightning is **electricity** let out by Earth's atmosphere. It usually happens during thunderstorms. Small drops of water and bits of ice inside clouds have electric charges. Some of these charges are positive and some are negative.

Make the Grade

An electric charge is an amount of electricity in an object that has to do with its ability to push or pull other objects.

When there are too many negative charges in a cloud, positive charges form on the ground below the cloud. **Opposite** charges are drawn to each other. The negative charges in the cloud want to join the positive ones below.

Make the Grade

Lightning is most common in **tropical** places, but it can happen almost anywhere in the world.

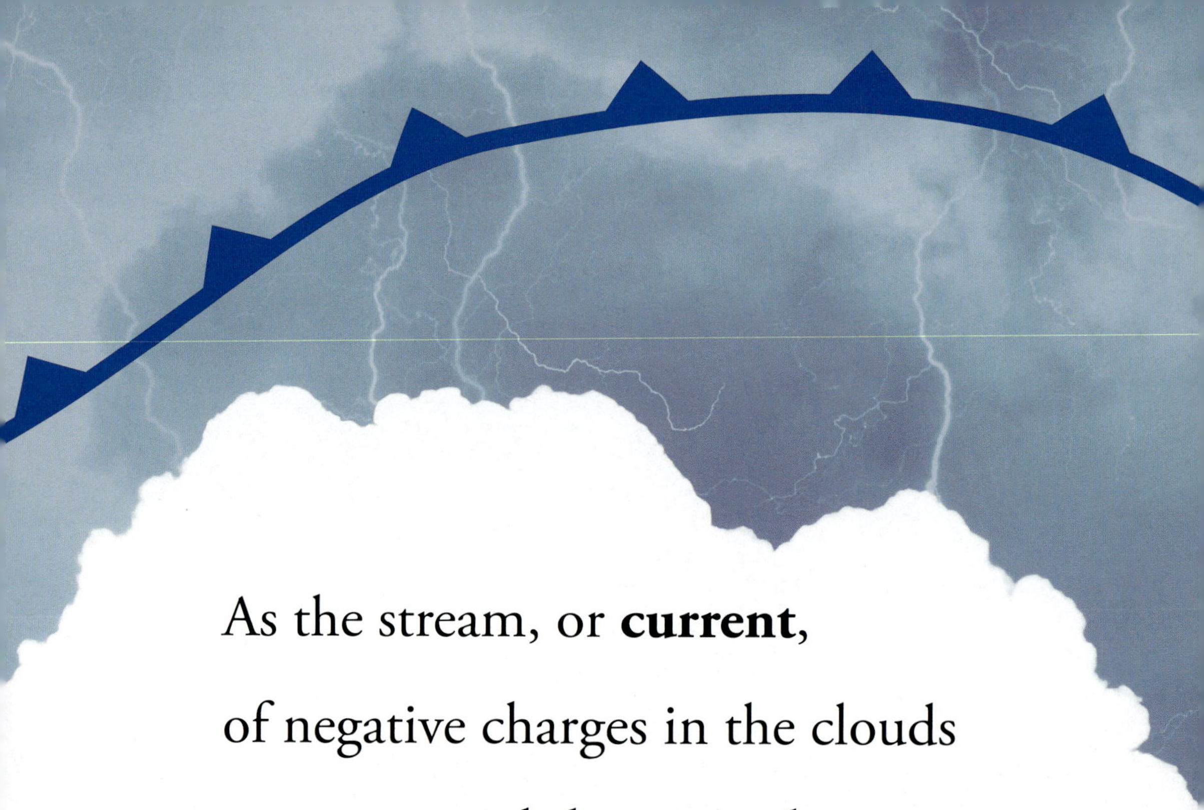

As the stream, or **current**, of negative charges in the clouds moves toward the ground, the positive current on the ground jumps to meet it. When the two currents meet, a flash of lightning happens. This happens again and again until the negative charges in the clouds are gone.

Make the Grade

Lightning does not always reach the ground. It can also happen within a cloud, between two or more clouds, or between a cloud and the air.

THINK ABOUT THUNDER

Lightning can make the air around it as hot as 54,000°F (30,000°C)! That much heat causes the gases in the air to expand, or get bigger. This is what creates the booming sound we know as thunder.

Make the Grade

Thunderstorms often have lots of wind. This is because of the movement of air from the lightning.

STORM SAFETY

The safest place to be during a thunderstorm is indoors. You should try to stay away from windows and doors. The biggest danger during a thunderstorm is lightning. Do not touch things that use electricity because lightning can travel through them.

Make the Grade

Do not take a bath or shower during a thunderstorm. In fact, try to stay away from any running water because lightning can travel through water pipes.

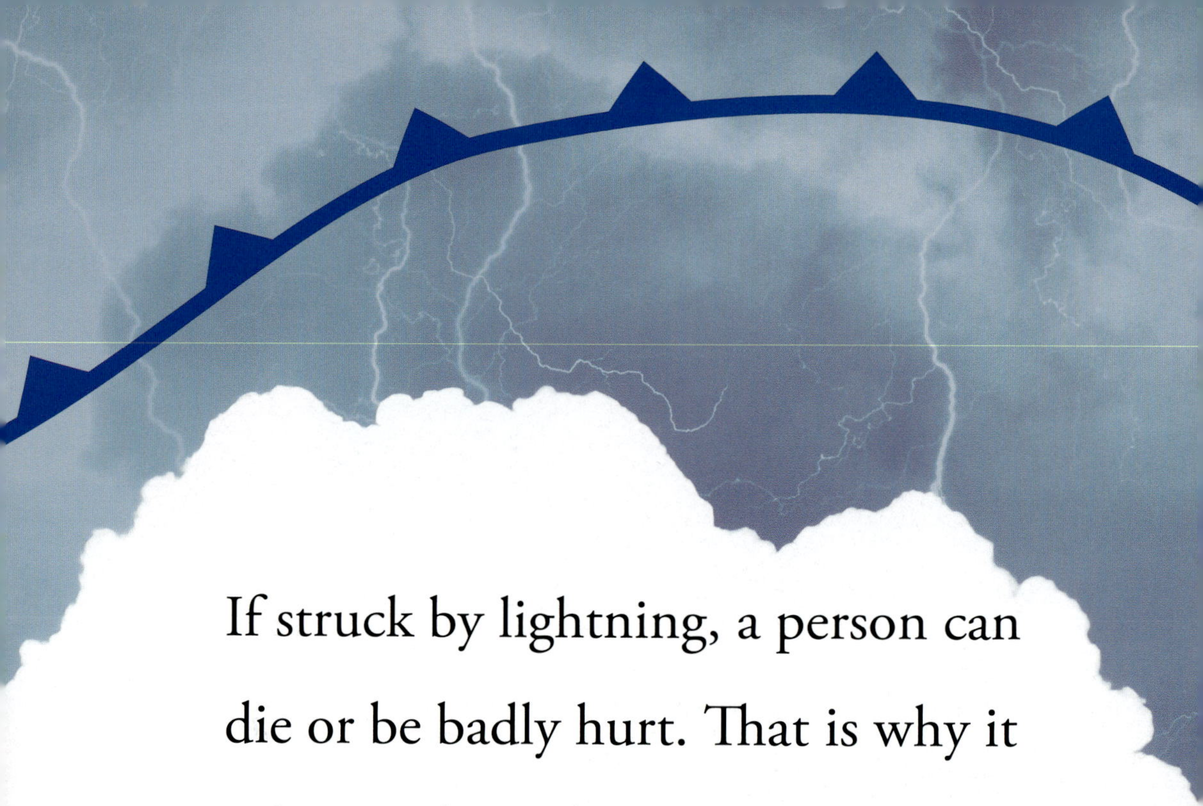

If struck by lightning, a person can die or be badly hurt. That is why it is best to be indoors. However, if someone is trapped outside during a thunderstorm, they should stay away from trees and water. They should also stay off hills or mountains.

Make the Grade

Lighting will commonly strike the tallest things around. That is why it is best to stay in low areas away from tall objects.

ALL ABOUT TIMING

If you have ever watched a thunderstorm, you may have noticed that you can see the lightning before you hear the thunder. However, these two things happen at about the same time. You just see the lightning first because light moves faster than sound.

Make the Grade

Light can move as fast as 186,000 miles (300,000 km) per second!

You can figure out about how far away lightning is by counting. After a lightning flash, start counting. Stop when you hear the thunder. **Divide** the number of seconds by five. That's about how many miles away from you the lightning was at the time you heard the thunder.

Make the Grade

Only try this from a safe place where you are not in danger from the thunderstorm. Do not stand right in front of a window to watch the lightning.

MAPPING THE STORM

The counting method gives you an idea of where the lightning was, but it is not exact. Scientists have tools that help them more closely map lightning. These tools can sense **radio waves** let out by currents in lightning storms.

Make the Grade

Lightning Mapping Arrays (LMA) are one way of tracking lightning. Scientists can use these systems to map thousands of points for one lightning flash to show where it formed.

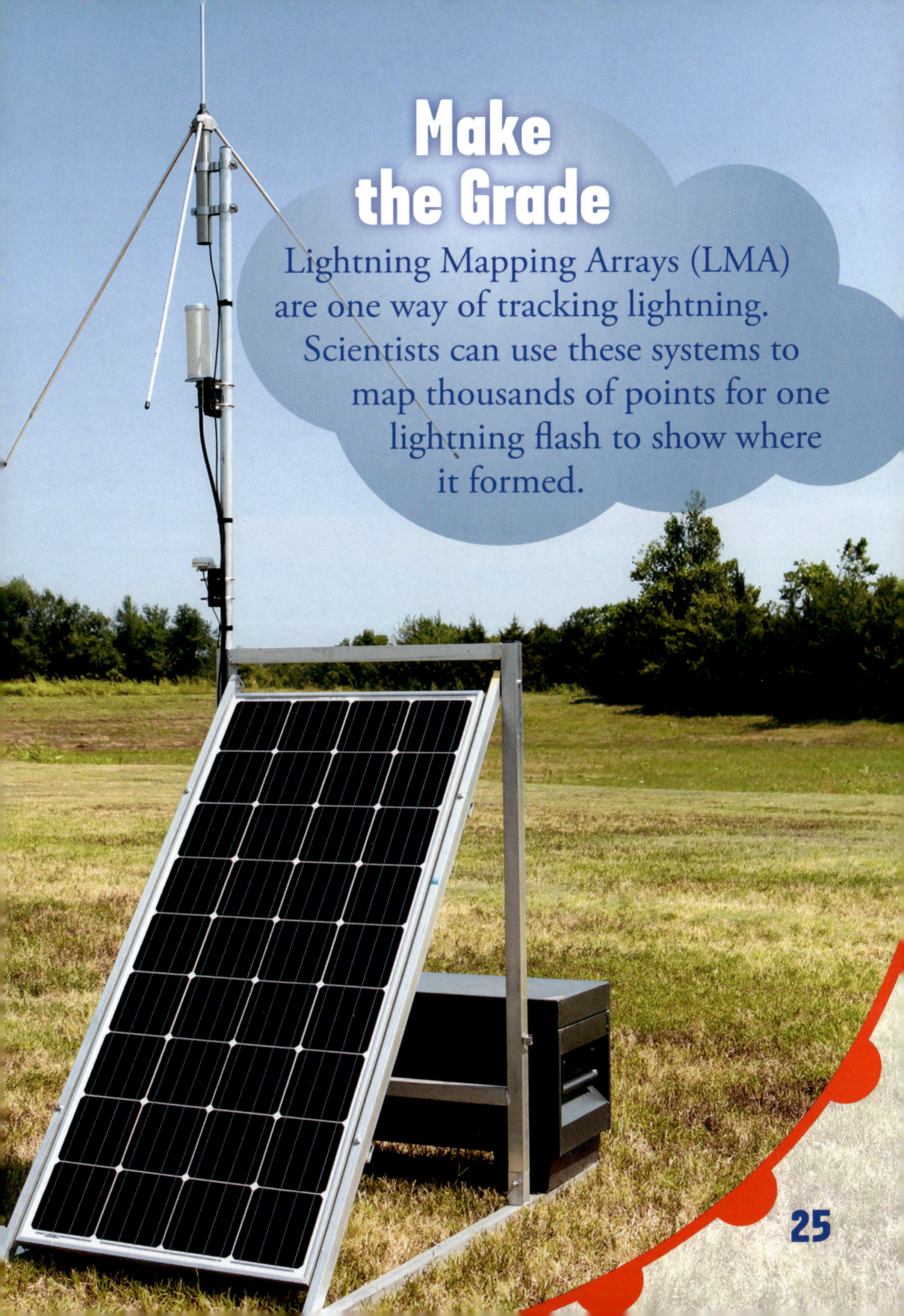

THUNDER AND LIGHTNING ALL OVER

Thunderstorms happen in most of the world. Near the **equator**, it is not uncommon for places to have more than 180 days with thunder each year. As you are reading this, there are likely more than 1,800 thunderstorms happening around the world!

Make the Grade

Scientists have guessed that about 8 million flashes of lightning happen every day!

Thunder and lightning are very common, but they are also very unsafe. Thunderstorms can lead to floods, **tornadoes**, and strong winds. People can get hurt and buildings can be destroyed. Listen to those in charge when they give directions on how to stay safe during thunderstorms.

Make the Grade

Each year in the United States, lightning hits the ground about 25 million times.

WAYS TO STAY SAFE IN A STORM

If there is ever thunder and lightning near you:

- Stay indoors.
- Stay away from doors and windows.
- Do not use running water.
- Do not touch anything that uses electricity.
- If you're trapped outdoors, stay away from tall objects and water.

GLOSSARY

current: A flow of electricity resulting from the movement of particles such as electrons.

divide: To break up evenly.

electricity: A form of energy found in nature that can also be artificially produced, such as by rubbing together two unlike things.

equator: An imaginary line around Earth that is the same distance from the North and South Poles.

opposite: Completely different.

radio wave: An electromagnetic wave with radio frequency.

rumble: To make a low, heavy rolling sound.

tornado: A violent whirling wind accompanied by a funnel-shaped cloud that moves in a narrow path over land.

tropical: Having to do with the warm parts of Earth near the equator.

FOR MORE INFORMATION

BOOKS

Farndon, John, Sean Callery, and Miranda Smith. *Weather*. New York, NY: Scholastic, 2020.

Johanson, Paula. *Lightning and Thunder*. New York, NY: Britannica Educational Publishing, 2019.

WEBSITE

Thunder and Lightning
scied.ucar.edu/learning-zone/storms/thunder-and-lightning
Find out more about thunder and lightning on this page.

Publisher's note to educators and parents: Our editors have carefully reviewed these websites to ensure that they are suitable for students. Many websites change frequently, however, and we cannot guarantee that a site's future contents will continue to meet our high standards of quality and educational value. Be advised that students should be closely supervised whenever they access the internet.

INDEX